♥

Something for Everyone, With Love

Jeanette Dowdell

iUniverse, Inc.
New York   Bloomington

Something for Everyone, With Love

Copyright © 2010 by Jeanette Dowdell

iUniverse books may be ordered through booksellers or by contacting:

iUniverse
1663 Liberty Drive
Bloomington, IN 47403
www.iuniverse.com
1-800-Authors (1-800-288-4677)

ISBN: 978-1-4502-2790-2 (pbk)
ISBN: 978-1-4502-2452-9 (ebk)
ISBN: 978-1-4502-2453-6 (hbk)

Printed in the United States of America
iUniverse rev. date: 5/25/10

*Forgiveness is the fragrance the violet
sheds on the heel that has crushed it.*

—Anonymous

PREFACE

This writing for me is actually a *"Pre ... Face."* It will tell you who I am, and give me a chance to show my "face"---- publicly for the first time.

When you have finished reading my work, I hope you will have a good idea of who I am. That will be my *"Post ... Face."* And hopefully, it will be just the beginning of a very long relationship.

Be forewarned, I enjoy writing about many subjects, but I find *time* to be the most fascinating. After all, time and life are synonymous. So you will find a preponderance of poems addressing this subject scattered throughout this work.

I would like to spend some time with you, and have you spend some time with me. And if it be so, it will please me greatly to know that I have pleased you with my thoughts and words. Now, speaking of time, enough said. Enjoy!

DEDICATION

I lovingly dedicate this work to those who knew me best:

Mabel G. Barton Dowdell, mother

John R. Dowdell, brother

ACKNOWLEDGMENTS

Eileen Obser, mentor

Many thanks for your friendship, encouragement, guidance and
for generously sharing your knowledge and expertise

My Friends

Those who not only listened, but heard, and offered never
ending support and encouragement

Ruth and Nunzio D'Anieri; ACE; Ann Glorioso; Florence E.
and William V. Facibene; Mabel M. Graf; Marilyn Ike; Judy K.
Meserve; Ruth B. Overton; Mary Reid; Kenneth Smith;
Marie Tonnesen; Dorothy F. Welenc

CONTENTS

MY WRITER'S DREAM

Like spring, I will burst upon the scene
To bring to life my writer's dream.
I will sleep no more, like winter gathering its fury,
Nor will I of the season be the judge and jury,
I will in fall feel its warmth, find countless joy in each
golden leaf,
And learn like poets of centuries past to be succinct, brief,
For too many words can clog the mind like twigs in a
stream,
And, I like summer in all its glory, will fulfill

MY WRITER'S DREAM

THE SPIRIT WHO STOKES THE FIRES

My words belong to God,
Creator of all life, sky, water, and sod,
From where else can thoughts such as these emanate?
So many words, poems, stories to create,
An endless pit for sharing,
Declaring, daring, and caring,
Ready on a moment's notice to set a tone,
Ready on a moment's notice to tweak, or moan and groan,
Always waiting to let the world know where it's at,
In a quiet, profound, explanatory chat,
To teach and give food for thought and action,
Seeing and hearing to point of distraction.
I feel the words are not always mine.
They are too often too apropos and fine.
Can they actually belong to me?
I feel they do not, you see,
Therefore, I honor the giver, the one who inspires,

"THE SPIRIT WHO STOKES THE FIRES"

"FLIGHT OF BIRDS"

Light as a feather, the flight of my words,
They sometimes compare to the flight of birds,
They glide and flow high into another world,
As my thoughts and sentences evolve, are unfurled,
And I am delighted beyond belief,
For I feel a sense of tremendous relief,
Memories and thoughts rattling within, screaming, "Let me out
to be what I can be,"
It's almost as though they are fighting an endless battle to be free.
Therefore, my words do fly like birds in flight,
Sometimes reaching inexplicable height
So move over, my fine feathered friends,
While I fly with you, sweet sparrows and wrens
My words will tell how you float and swoop and glide,
And give us all an unreachable world in which to hide,
As we, with eye and mind, find comfort and peace in your ways,
Looking heavenward into a sky that never ceases to amaze,
We are so lucky to share your flight,
No cost—absolute delight
So, I take to the sky, fly with you; I hope you don't mind.
Where else can my thoughts and words such freedom find?
Yes, there is a freedom flight to my words
That can be found in the

"FLIGHT OF BIRDS"

"A POET"

Most people like to read poetry only if it suits their tastes, I find.
When they read prose, I often hear, "It's not rhymed,"
Sometimes, the bold of heart might say, "I don't get it, it's tripe,"
Should that poet bow, become contrite?
As a poet they can, if they're not resting in their little dirt bed,
However, their legacy may be published and praised after they're dead,
Then, they will live on and conquer their world
They'll share their very being, their words, as originally unfurled.
How often does one hear within, as they create, "It's not right, I
don't like it"?
Admittedly, all who create must be filled with grit;
Be ready to hear the truth, even if it does hurt.
Then consider, who in your circle can be declared expert?
Keep in mind, what delights one may never delight another.
Listen, re-evaluate, but never give up, brother.
Poetry cannot always be the lightest of muse events
Some poems are so deep; they need analysis, ladies and gents.
All meaning rests within the minds of its creator and muse
For me, some things I can understand and enjoy, but please
don't deliberately bemuse,
So now, I leave you with this thought: write and think, and
think and write, sun up to sunset,
And follow me, for someday I will be

"A POET"

"WAS I BORN ON TIME?"

We don't choose our time to be born
It's predetermined
By whom, however?
Is there a list that goes back to creation—day one?
Throughout my lifetime, many have said, "When your time is
up, it's up."
Your name is in the "Big Book."
Given that, our beginning must also have been recorded,
A time to start, and a time to end,
A time to fill a specific timeframe in the evolution of time.
That's why there are generations born, one after another.
What a magnificent Plan—
Not just the evolution of man, but the multifaceted faces of all
the universes.
Have each of the planets in our universe experienced such an evolution?
Was there life on each that destroyed itself?
Rendering itself totally unrecognizable to each succeeding generation?
Was I born on time?
Am I accomplishing what I was born to accomplish?
Have I filled the slot—that infinitesimal portion of the greater
whole—that was mine to fill?
How wonderful to be part of something undefined, and still in
the process of being created,
To recognize where I fit in
To be one of the building blocks of an ongoing creation is unbelievable
Now, you know why I ask

"WAS I BORN ON TIME?"

"NEVER MORE CLOSE TO GOD"

Most cannot determine a moment of conception
But they welcome the state with an open heart reception.
A woman is never more close to God than at the moment she
conceives,
For the hand of God reaches down with the blessing she receives,
And her partner too, is not excluded from His Grace,
For part of him is part of the child he will embrace.
You cannot walk away, and simple say, "It's not mine."
God blessed you with a gift, blessed you with a new life divine,
And in that divinity He changed your fate
You must know that; you were partners in a sacred decision to
create
Do you have the right to destroy God's creation?
To rip the seed of life out of His hand? That's a colossal assumption.
Now you're in a new Garden of Eden; His trust is in you,
You've already by act thought it through; you've already made
your choice, haven't you?
It's not the time to change your mind, after the fact.
The best decisions are by most made before an act,
But when God is involved, don't you think it requires deeper
thought—more respect?
Who are you to negate His work, cast a wand of reject?
To act in such a manner appears odd,
When we're

"NEVER MORE CLOSE TO GOD"

"LIVING IN CAPTIVITY"

We live our lives in captivity,
Trapped in our mind's proclivity.
Most of us are creatures of habit, after all
We imitate and into total mental mimicry fall
How many thoughts in a day are original—different—new?
Consider the world's population: Even then, they offer few
From birth, are we taught to think, seek new vistas, and expand?
No, we live in the shadows of others; the "unstretchable" rubber
band.
What they see, we see; what they hear, we hear,
And all too often, what they believe, we believe; what they fear,
we fear.
How many ever truly break every mold?
We're born with souls already sold,
We're born into living captivity
Our thoughts, words, deeds, belong to others; an historical activity,
We are not who we are; we just think we are,
Think we are who we should be, are expected to be; how bizarre.
We live in and belong to our age; day after day, turning page
after page,
We live within the confines of its offerings most sage.
We can't live in another era.
Our story must unfold in the book of its time—a reflection in
that mirror.
To think otherwise is sheer folly, nonsensicality
Its aura will never change; it can't. It's living a perpetual captivity
We profess our options are limitless; they are not.
Much of our daily routine fits the category of "fairy-grot."
But what other options do we have; can we live in space?

Aren't we, after all, simply part of a human race?
We live accordingly, constantly shriveling our being with
unbridled selectivity,
Sadly remaining caged, accepting life as it is, unaware that we're

"LIVING IN CAPTIVITY"

"BORN TO DIE"

Never! It's illogical; it doesn't make sense,
And the reason is extremely intense
God doesn't make all flowers to pass on,
Nor does each tree of Creation fail to bloom after its bare
winter season's gone,
And humans, far more intricate, magnificent, and functionally
alert,
Must find a new life, a new time, after death to revert,
Revert back to whole, and perform once again on an upper plane,
Perhaps in a new form, perhaps not on Earth, simply angels to
console,
be reborn again,
To be spirits of action with good minds remaining intact,
To perform beyond today—filled with what we once did lack
There's no need, at death, to cry.
Given the depth of our Creation, we could never just be

"BORN TO DIE"

"LIFE"

The clock is life,
Living, breathing, moving away from each yesterday,
Awakening each tomorrow,
Relentlessly stealing time from all who hear it speak

"O SHADOW MINE"

Who Needs Whom?

Where are you, O shadow mine?
When the sun disappears, you do, too,
But, I know you're there; we intertwine.
We're so attached, I hear you coo.

What purpose do you serve my alter ego?
Others see you, but can't say why you're there.
Where I walk, how I stand, you remain "status quo,"
You could be so many things, as my body you share

Are you my guardian angel, my protector, my shield?
Don't answer that; it might frighten me to know,
But then again, it might frighten me more, send me afield,
If you were an apparition, a ghost all aglow

Somehow I feel that you serve a purpose,
Perhaps to lead me to my final rest,
Will we double a loss in Earth's census?
At my demise, will you make my trip "home" less the test?

Or, are you only a figment without reality?
We're joined from the feet up; does that mean my body you define?
You need me to exist, and light to find identity.
My lifetime defines yours,

"O SHADOW MINE"

"TAKE TIME"

Slow down!
Smell the roses—
That's sound advice,

But I smell the roses year round,
Not only when on the stem,
But in winter's chill and when the snow falls,

Anywhere,
Anytime,

Every time I take a deep breath,
I can smell roses within,

For they live in my heart,
Fragrant and sweet,

And I can call them at will,
To relive many precious moments, when I did

"TAKE TIME"

"THE WHITE ROSE"

An Illusion

The white rose exists only in each beholder's eye,
For purity and perfection are found only in God, not any magi
No one, not even a sorcerer, can create perfection in any form.
The white rose is only white in the hand of its Creator, at its dawn
Watch as its petals of velvet unfold at birth
As they gently roll upon themselves when presented on Earth.
At dawn and dust, the skin, soft and fresh, glows with the
reflected rays of the sun.
They're tainted, within and without, with the palest of hues;
their flesh is overrun.

It's an illusion, perceived as not being refined, while bud to
blossom it grows
It's an illusion, as close to white as the purity of soul

"THE WHITE ROSE"

"TOUCHED BY THE HAND OF GOD— TOUCHED BY LOVE"

"What is love?"
Ask a million people, and you'll receive a million answers,
But rarely will you hear,
"God is love,
Therefore, we are love."
After all, we are made in His image
He is the Spirit of our flesh
How, then, can we be less than love?
Love is profound, yet simple
It is delicate, yet strong
It is forgiving
It is beautifully unforgettable—everlasting
To live love is to know love,
Its weaknesses and its strengths,
But it can only be known by its giving and receiving.
Love is infinite,
And within its own state of intangibility rests its mystery,
But there is no mystery about the fact that each conception is a
testimony to love,
For without the love of God, we would not have received the
gift of life.
We all were, without question, at birth,

"TOUCHED BY THE HAND OF GOD— TOUCHED BY LOVE"

"YES, IT IS A MATTER OF CHOICE"

BEFORE and AFTER

HOW MANY SAVIORS HAVE BEEN DESTROYED?

Yes, it's a matter of choice,
And in the wilderness there cries a voice,
"Is it all a matter of belief?
Is it all a matter of instant relief?"
Ask any woman who cannot conceive
What gift she would most like to receive.
Daily, worldwide, abortions women hail,
Second coming—how many saviors have found "the pail?"
We'll never know; we give embryos no choice.
They lose their lives, and are given no voice.
Perhaps God has sent another Virgin Mary to save the World—
the earth,
And she too was discarded in an aborted birth.
The World in its present day agony and pain
Shows no perceptive slowing toward change, or wane
It continues to travel on a tawdry course,
With no thought given to ways of shame, or remorse,
And the answer is simple in this case.
It's a matter of will, strength, desire, choice—before and after
you embrace.
You are the result of your mother's choice; you're alive—you live.
Your turn; you have a choice—life to take, life to give.
The Virgin Mary heard God's call; today, the decision is yours—
do you drown sin with your voice?
There's a right, and there's a wrong, and

"YES, IT IS A MATTER OF CHOICE"

"A LIFETIME JOB"

A sperm,
An egg,
Sex, with or without, love,
A baby

"TEARS—DIAMONDS OF LIFE"

Tears of … *joy*,
Tears of … *sorrow*,
Tears in … *reserve*,
Tears for … *extinguishing*

"THE FIRES OF TOMORROW"

"IT'S A JOURNEY WORTH TAKING"

From the first breath until the last,
It's a journey worth taking.
The learning, the doing, the dying,
The caring, the giving, the sharing,
The love on all planes,
The good days and the bad,
What's one without the other?
The surprises, the excitement,
The reflective quiet moments,
The joy, the sorrow,
The tears that express both,
The laughter, which makes the heavens swell with joy,
The failures, the successes, humble pride,
The sweet gentle hand of a child in ours,
Nurturing, maturing, becoming one in spirit,
Giggles, smiles, and heartwarming thoughts,
Being thankful for the rising sun,
The moon and stars that shine,
And the best gift of all,
The strength to live each day of our life,
So it can be said,

"IT'S A JOURNEY WORTH TAKING"

"THANK YOU, O MOTHER MINE"

O, mother mine, filled with warm, loving, and tender care,
I know your deeds have brought you angel wings to wear.
I also know you would hate the thought of that,
For you always said you wanted to reside in the "hot habitat,"
Where all your friends and the "fun and frolic" would be,
But your life was one of giving and sharing, lived unselfishly,

So I think that you are now comfortably at rest,
Because you did more than your share, more than your best
Surprising, some have criticized your ways, even though they
were close to you
They publicly exposed the faults they knew,
But faults can be washed away by measures of good,
Something that those who could only tear down never
understood

Their minds and hearts resided on the dark side of life.
They lived not to love, show care and concern, but to cause
strife.
Most knew their ways; their beastly role,
Knew, too, the bells of love for them would never toll.
So you see, I only want to remember the multitudinous good in
your lifetime,
As I proudly and lovingly say,

"THANK YOU, O MOTHER MINE"

"ONE HUNDRED ELEVEN"

Mom—October 8, 1897–August 6, 1974

Memories can be beautiful and sweet
When they recall special moments in repeat
Death, "It's a seven day wonder," my mom used to say,
But had she lived, she'd be one hundred eleven today.
It has never been a seven-day wonder, her passing,
For her life was filled with solid memories, die-casting.
She was the most unselfish person I have ever known,
But she was surrounded by takers, all selfish to the bone
Living her way, everyone else always came first,
With never a "how about me?" outburst,
She accepted life as it came down the road,
And met all the challenges, met every heavy load.
She was very sentimental, filled with warmth and love,
The family peacemaker, ever the true loving dove.
So it's easy to recall with birthday wishes of old,
A life that should be remembered, never to go untold,
And forget the death "wonder days" numbering seven.
I still celebrate in memory her birthday—Yep!

"ONE HUNDRED ELEVEN"

"WE WILL WALTZ AGAIN"

In Memoriam—J. R. Dowdell, brother

There comes a time when we all must part;
That is known from the very start
But when loved ones leave, they rarely leave the heart
Memory upon memory the mind continues to impart
My brother was the last to travel to the Great Beyond
His memories still flood my mind, memories of which I am
most fond
One, however, shines the brightest by far:
The dancing we did in our youth, star to star,
Gliding and floating in heaven to each refrain
Those memories remain and recur, and someday I know

"WE WILL WALTZ AGAIN"

"HAPPINESS"

Written for my friend Mabel

Happiness is a state of mind
To live it, is knowing what is kind
A mental cathartic, gentle and sweet,
It lifts the emotions, sends tensions into retreat
When we are under its spell, we hold fast, wishing it never to end,
Knowing full well the reverse is bound to descend
Everyone works hard to avoid and shed the woes,
But that's how we all learn, and how one grows
Who wouldn't want constant happiness with its serenity and bliss?
That's when time should stand still, and not to mention this
would be remiss
When happiness abounds, we all secretly cry, "Don't go away,"
For it's in that state we wish to stay
Don't burst the bubble and shatter the warm feelings deep,
For we do not wish to be engulfed in sadness—to weep,
"O, happiness, don't move on, stay, stay,
Stay with us, do, just for another day—another day."
But then again, without darkness we would never know
happiness to be so bright,
And without the cold dark night, we would never feel the
warmth of each day's light,
So when darkness comes, know happiness will return; it will rise,
For it's a state of mind, waiting in the wings to shout, "Hello,
surprise!"

Waiting to lift our spirits in a multitude of ways,
Waiting to lift us up, carry us through the mean days.
So, be assured, the happiness state of mind will return full of cheerfulness,
Then it's up to you to latch on and enjoy each moment of

"HAPPINESS"

"LIFE IS MUSIC"

For Florence Facibene, who selected the word "music" to
commemorate the appearance of her granddaughter, Zoe,
with the Nassau All-County Chorus

Life is music with all its tones,
Even creaky sounds like the motion of old bones
A squeaky door comes alive and makes itself known,
When it's very movement cries out with a groan.
The wind whistles and creates a distinct sound
As it swirls and curls, reaching up to heaven, down to the ground
The birds chirp, the frogs croak, the bees buzz,
Everything filled with life and breath, plus, does
Can that be so? The crows caw, horses whinny, and cows moo
Open your mouth and sometimes there can be music too
When life, breath, music, and sound come together,
Are they not the proverbial "birds of a feather?"
Stars twinkle to their own beat,
Tapping toes mean the beat has reached the feet
What doesn't have a sound?
Listen up, look around,
Give life a chance to show its stuff
After all, it's still a diamond in the rough.
Squirrels and chipmunks chatter, cats meow and purr,
Bears grunt, owls hoot; sounds all, whether feather or fur,
Waterfalls rumble, streams ripple and surfs swish,
Chickens cackle, bull's snort, pigs oink before they reach your dish,
Snakes hiss, ants hum, roosters crow "good morning,"
Dogs, beloved pets and faithful friends, bark their warning,

Lions roar, elephants mournfully cry, flocks of birds tunefully
flap their wings
Sound all; music to the ears; nature sings
And you think a sharp or a flat is very natural,
Perhaps, but I can't make that factual,
But eighth, quarter, half, or whole notes in their proper place
Will bring serenity, calmness, and a smile to everyone's face
Music, like guns and war, can shatter sound,
But its affect most often lead to deeper love, a life more profound.
The music of life is a true concert, if only we hear,
But if all the sounds are intermingled, that's disharmony, I fear
So, in this life, let's pick the parts that in harmony ring,
Bring all peoples together in peace and joy to sing
If taken in proper perspective, your last breath can true life be,
Because for you, it will open a new world not all can see,
For I believe, even in death, the music in silence plays on
As our souls search and reach for heaven and the great beyond.
There's more music in silence than meets the mind,
For in silence, music can sometimes be the most kind,
And, if we choose to let it be,

"LIFE IS MUSIC"

"AJ"

Who is AJ?
I can't tell; she won't let me say,
But the letter "A" stands for angel
She deserves a classical wreath of laurel;
She helps others without telling a soul
She smiles, cooks, cleans, shops, and she's there to console.
Oh, how I wish I could walk in those shoes,
Albeit my own size, if I could choose
Her problems remain her problems—go without note
There is no ego; no need to say, "I did this or that"; no need to
gloat
A drive to a bookstore, a visit at home, a walk on the beach,
Always giving, satisfying someone else's desire, living constantly
within outreach,
But only others who live within the realm of her kind way
Have the right to evaluate, share, have something to say,
Never looking for applause, thanks, recognition, or rewards,
That's the persona we all should strive towards
So, as much as I want to point out good deeds and shout,
"Hurray!"
The spotlight, I know, would not be appreciated by

"AJ"

"24 HOURS?"

8,760 hours in a 365-day year,
8,784 hours in a 366-day Leap Year,
So, why do 24 hours come and go so quickly?
If we live to age 70, we will have lived 629,400 hours.
What is 24 hours, when compared to 70 years' worth?
It's like a grain of sand on a beach.
Ponder then, the minute, speedy little devil.
It moves like a wink.
In 70 years, we squander 38, 556 of those little suckers,
And we note how quickly the days fly,
My, my ...
Now consider the second, $1/60^{th}$ of a minute.
How quick are they.
In 70 years, we dance through 2,313,360,000 seconds,
And we still question the quickness of a day.
It's all relative, isn't it?
I found the answer to, "Where does the time go?"
It travels at its own pace, not ours,
And it slips into oblivion,
As we do, when we say our final good-bye
I wonder if we'll meet again (time and I), as we travel in the
great beyond?
As we explore, together, our timeless tomorrows?
Compared to a lifetime, how long is

"24 HOURS?"

"CAN YOU?"

Can you create a butterfly?
A fly?
A flea?
Anything?
A bird on the wing?

Can you create a leaf—elm, maple, oak?
A tree?
A flower?
Anything?
A bird on the wing?

Can you create a stream, a lake, an ocean?
A natural waterfall?
A raindrop?
Anything?
A bird on the wing?

Can you create anything from its source?
Can you create
A bird on the wing?

"CAN YOU?"

"WALKING ON A TREE"

Without a doubt, few think about the tree beneath their feet,
Or the beauty that it provides, that's truly neat.
When the Indians and Pilgrims walked this land,
The soil was what they had to rest upon, and stand.
It was surely damp and cold, uninviting, too,
Yet the early scouts loved the mantle of stars and the beauty of dew.
It's told, time and time again in each old American frontier story,
Nature's beauty, creation, oh, the glory,
Then came modern times, and the more sophisticated we grew,
And as we learned to build, old timers gave up the soil they knew.
Wood was no longer gathered for the hearth's fire,
It was gathered to build the cabins, and today, the grand
hardwood floors to admire.
So, when you look down and see the beauty of oak,
Remember where it came from, and the one-time shade of its
cloak.
They're a treasure, whether over head or under foot, you see,
And thank them dearly, each time you realize that you're

"WALKING ON A TREE"

"FRIENDS"

Love given, love taken, love shared—
Love never ends,
Because we were and are what we were and are,
And will always be—

"FRIENDS"

"A TUGGING AT THE HEART"

When friends are far apart,
There is a tugging at the heart.
They would rather be together to laugh and chat,
Even if only about this and that.
It can be very lonesome when good friends go;
Some do, without a choice, you know
They fly far away into another day,
Or simply travel their life's way
The heart always holds a chamber for special friends,
For the memories, and love, never ends,
Any quiet moment of any given day, one can recall
Moments of grief, moments of joy, great and small,
Shared and blessed by each other's need,
Remembered forever; a warm, loving deed,
But there's one thing to be said, when friends are far apart:
With true friends, no matter where they are, there will always be

"A TUGGING AT THE HEART"

"THE BOW"

In memory of my friends Iris R. Hannon and Lois A. Tator

Three lives wrapped around one bow—
That sounds silly, I know,
And I can't even remember when it all began,
But I do recall the last to receive it became its annual custodian
It became a real treasure down through the years
It provided joy and laughter, and carried us through sorrows
and tears,
And the story is probably as silly as the premise upon which it is
based
I gave my friend, Lois, a birthday gift upon which the bow was
placed
It was very unusual; a beautiful shade of blue
I really didn't want to give it away; that was true,
And when my friend, Iris, saw it, she cried, "I want the bow."
It was the only one of that color in the store; otherwise, I would
have come home with a ton in tow.
Lois was laughing, saying, "Hey, it's my package, my bow, my gift,"
And she knew that I wanted it back, too; get the drift?
But she was generous to a fault; she could never be that mean;
the fun grew,
So as friends, we discussed the situation—as grown-ups do,
But no one would give in.
Obviously, Lois was the birthday girl, so she should win,
But our final resolution turned out to be the best; it was
simple—we'll share,
And so it became a treasure to three friends who never forgot to
care.

Now just how can you share a bow?
Lois promised to put that bow on one of Iris' packages; her
birthday was next in line,
And Iris then, would place it on a package next year when the
celebration was mine,
And down through the years, it became a special joy on each
celebrant's day,
But as time went on, it began to look as old as it was, flat and
faded, but it never did fray.
On about one hundred and five birthday packages that bow was
tied,
And when I recently found it in the bottom of one of my
moving boxes, I cried.
Did I toss it away?
You bet your life I didn't; to my death it will stay
Its history, its memories, make it a treasure,
Everyone can laugh if they want, my pleasure,
For it will still be bringing some joy, a little fun
Now, don't we all need that when each day is done?
We all agreed each year to let the love and sentiments attached
to this simple gem grow,
But somehow our age took away its frivolity; it remained
however, deeply cherished—

"THE BOW"

"MY LITTLE ONE, MY LITTLE JOHN"

With love for John Emmet Sikorski, Jr., now age five

Yes, Little John, I called upon the spirits of those past.
Rarely do I ever disturb their rest, which should be undisturbed
and last,

But for you, a child of love who was so very ill,
I could not conceive of waiting and standing still.

Two churches of mine, one past and one present, were asked for
prayer
Everyone responded, almost in unison to show how they did care.

Neighbors, friends, former business associates, and fellow
students were advised
They all lifted up their voices to the heavens, the skies.

And so, day after day, we waited for reports about you.
It's so difficult, when there is nothing anyone can do.

But faith and prayer strengthened not only you, but each of us,
As we placed you in your Creator's hands with full trust

Only He can give you what you need to breath and grow,
Because you are special, Little John; this should tell you so

Today, all thoughts are with you; you're twelve days old,
And you may be removed from the respirator, I'm told

What good news for all to hear,
But you are on your own now, my little dear

You can handle it, and I hope the pain is gone
You've just got to see this through,

"MY LITTLE ONE, MY LITTLE JOHN"

"HOW OLD IS TIME?"

Time has no age, or value, without the existence of everything
that moves, grows, succeeds, and lives within its metered web.
—Jeanette Dowdell

In the beginning …
Really?
Time could have existed before the beginning …
It's possible.
Tell me, did the Big Bang take place *on time, in time?*
Or did the Big Bang create time?
Does time live on time?
Does time create its own time?
Does time keep time?
Does time ever tire?
Maybe when it slows down for us on occasion,
Is time actually what we perceive time to be?
Profound fact: For us, time begins at birth and dies at death …
Or does it?
All things are part of time,
But what is time a part of?
There's a time to sow,
There's a time to reap,
There's a time to be born,
There's a time to die,

There's a time to do this,
There's a time to do that,
There's time,
And then …
There's no time.

"HOW OLD IS TIME?"

"A CONVERSATION WITH LILLIAN"

A Precious Moment in Time

ONE THANKSGIVING DAY: No matter the year ... It's the moment that counts

A simple chore, a statement of love,
My friend Marilyn's Mom, Lillian,
The matriarch of a wonderful family,
Stood at the sink and insisted she wash the pots.
Forget the dishwasher,
She had her own built-in variety—
Two hands,
Those pots shone brighter than any modern convenience could
have turned out,

It was Thanksgiving Day
And I could tell that she was thankful to be part of the
wonderful festivities that surrounded her.
Her children and grandchildren, those who could make it, were
present,
Guests and family treated as one,
Smiles all the way around, but none broader than Lillian's,
In her mind, her eighty-plus years did not bring special
privileges,
She wanted to be useful,
So she demonstrated her zest for life without wearing it for all
to see,
Quietly, she went about her business.
Quietly, she scrubbed and washed the pots.

Nothing new for her; she raised five children.

I joined her to dry her trophies of pleasure,
"Lillian," I asked, "Aren't you tired?"
"A little, but I'll sit down when the pots are done."
She not only said it, but said it with a twinkle in her eyes
And a broad smile upon her lips
I could tell that she was contented
She felt at that moment that life was good
If I could have read her mind, I'm sure she was thinking,
"What more could I possibly ask for?
Thank you, God."
I can picture that scene as though it was yesterday, not five plus
years past

In a crowd of Thanksgiving revelers, we stood in our own little
world
We talked about days gone by as we watched the sunset
An airplane whizzed by, landing gear down
We both agreed that some other loved ones were making their
journey home
We chatted, laughed, and wished for the best of years past.
Reminiscing will do that,
But for me, one of the best parts of that Thanksgiving Day remains

"A CONVERSATION WITH LILLIAN—

A Precious Moment in Time"

"KINDNESS"

*Special thanks to Mary Reid
for her friendship and constant help!*

There is no payment equal to kindness that I know
The heart is larger in those who behave so.
Their deeds are not always rewarded in kind,
They have a wonderful empathetic way set in their mind,
They know the value of a sweet word, a smile, a gentle touch,
Somehow, they find joy in their own actions, which may appear
little, but mean so much,
Don't ever change a thing; keep doing what you do,
For I know a great reward will be yours when you're through
You will be entitled to nothing less
For constantly giving love through your

"KINDNESS"

"AN ABORTED EMBRYO SPEAKS"

What could I have been …?
What should I have been …?
What am I now …?

PRO-CHOICE:

ALWAYS COMES WITH A CRITICAL DECISION
BEFORE, AND WITH A MORE CRITICAL OPTION
AFTER

PRO-LIFE:

ALWAYS COMES WITH THE SAME OPTION, BEFORE
AND AFTER

"AN EMBRYO'S CRY"

(A Stem Cell Controversy)

As the embryo said, "It might be controversial,
but it's a matter of life and death …MINE."
—Jeanette Dowdell

"Hear me, please do,
I live, I am; remove me and my life is through.
I'd like to know what I could become,
Frolicsome, irksome, troublesome, venturesome—perhaps
welcome
I would like a chance to be who I am … me,
Not in a pail just above the floor and below someone's knee,
I don't understand the logic—to save a life, you'll take mine,
Dichotomous thinking, at the very best—hard to define,
You're saving a life lived, now chosen by its creator to move on,
Angel wings or devil's tails to don,
Give me the same opportunity of life; to live—to be
Selfless, not selfish, thinking life is guaranteed and pain free
There's got to be a better way,
Think on, oh geniuses of today,
Abortion is not always an answer either; it's too easy to destroy,
To play God, be a self-appointed life envoy.
A seed is planted and it begins to grow—
That's a sign of life, don't you know?

It's so easy to pull a plant from the ground, or a cell from an
animal womb,
There's no resistance in this action of pre-determined doom.
It's so easy to perform such deeds, but why?
Stop! Listen! Hear me, please do,"

"AN EMBRYO'S CRY"

"THE MIND"

The mind—the mind,
How shallow—how deep,
Powerful and intricate,
Our storage bin for minutiae,
Interlocking rails with constantly moving impulses,
Yet, how little we know about what marks its winding trails,
How much of our living has been sucked into its black hole?
Gone forever?
I wonder.
Recorded for posterity?
Who knows?
Ah, those who have joined the Eternal Elite,
Does our first breath of death trigger an instant replay of our
life?
Where do our memories rest?
Those powerful thoughts that are strong enough to visit at will,
Where are they after death?
Do they take their place on the re-run tape?
Right now, while living, I would like to travel my mind's road
back to its inception,
Journey from millisecond one to the present
How long would that journey take?
I'd like to live my life in each "what if" scenario.
I'd like to know why I made each decision as made,
And what would each secondary decision have looked like.
It would be a fantastic journey; long, involved—fantastic.

The mind goes beyond just a magnificent creation.
It's an undefined infinite—seldom recognized for what it is—
The Alpha and Omega,
The absolute essential,

"THE MIND"

"EMBERS TO FLAME"

So many long for fame,
They hunger for the world to know their name,
Some struggle mightily to be heard—to be seen.
What is the trophy they wish to glean?
Ideas must be shared; they are not simply embers for the mind
Waiting to break loose, to change the ways of humankind
Ideas are like dust—ever present, ever near.
Where would we be without those who dwell upon the new,
change old and murky to clear?
How many embers of the mind have remained trapped?
Waiting for a lifetime to be unwrapped?
We'll never know, because they stayed in the gray matter of the
brain,
Never to be released across an educational plane.
They remain, and remain, and remain—
What they are, never to change from

"EMBERS TO FLAME"

"THE ULTIMATE WEAPON
of DESTRUCTION"

Teeth?
Stones and rocks?
Clubs, axes, and knives?
Spears and swords?
Bows and arrows?

Catapults?
Cannons?
Guns—single shot/multi-shot?
The Gatling?
Rifles and machine guns?

Gas?
Big guns?
Atom bombs?
Hydrogen bombs?
Scatter bombs?
Missiles?

Biological agents?
Chemical agents?

NO!
THE HUMAN MIND
IS

"THE ULTIMATE WEAPON
of DESTRUCTION"

"WE ARE RIVALS!"

**What does the word WAR mean?
Simply,**

"We Are Rivals!"

"PEACE"

Just look around …
It's not to be found;
Wherever does it hide?
War always looms, as close as any flowing tide,
For there are those who are born to every generation who stir
turmoil,
Those who keep Earth's cauldron turned to boil,
Peace brings less to the coffers of the greedy,
Turn the tide; let's face it, there will always be needy,
Peace is a dream we chase,
And if we are lucky, we'll win the race.
We'll live in the shadows of the next coming war
Until we reach the end of our life's tether; close our life's door.
How many generations have actually lived without war?
Has anyone recorded for posterity that score?
Preparations for, and wars themselves, never cease,
It's a travesty of justice, a whistling in the dark,

"PEACE"

"IT MUST BE IN THE WATER"

I've listened to politicians for years,
They smile, and lie, and lie, and lie, to cover up their fears,
It's obvious; they don't know what they're doing,
But they're surrounded by many others who join their cooing.
They are all afraid that John/Jane Q. Public might uncover the truth,
They suffer perpetual pain, and it's not coming from a bad tooth,
It's coming from all the "hidden agendas" they espouse,
Knowing their constituencies would not agree with the flagrant crap they house,
One politician is equal to another.
They all come from the same place, a loving woman, called mother,
I guarantee they're not honest with them either; their once upon a time—
sweet little eager beavers,
For their nature changes as soon as they sit in the Chambers of Deceivers.
It is like a plague; it corrupts their very being.
They're despised by the good guys, who step aside all knowing and seeing.
Few, I fear, are able to resist, as they "oughter."
By God, quick, someone call a plumber,

"IT MUST BE IN THE WATER"

Lie detector tests are always an option

"THE CONGRESSIONAL MASSACRE"

The Demise of All Professional Political Pinocchios

A full congressional meeting was held in Washington, DC., today,
And all members of both Houses were stabbed to death—no
one got away.
Who was responsible? Who perpetrated that act?
That was easy to determine; it was evident, in fact,
Given the reason, all their noses were Pinocchioesque,
They stabbed each other; it must have been quite burlesque,
Their operational ways finally caught up with them,
Saying one thing, doing another, conniving; the aisles strewn
with each diadem
Their noses had turned sharp; they were now steel.
That's how their lying, selfish ways led to their deaths; that was
real.
In the future to avoid such a disaster, note, not "tragedy," my
friends.
All who wish to serve, and do serve, must submit to lie detector
tests, during and before one ascends and descends.
That would curb any misdeeds, and any germinated ill
conceived conspired acts over time.
For today, it's too easy to satisfy paid constituents' demands in
the present congressional clime,
We've seen it time and time again, is that not so?
The longer they remain on their tufted seats, illegalities seem to
grow, and grow, and grow,
"We the People," the majority, are left out in the cold.
We don't decide what's right, for the "good" of most—no, that's
left to a handful of controlling bold,

49

And so a far "Superior Power" had enough, and labeled each lie
with a physical change.
Apparently, there were no exceptions on the law producing range.
With each lie, their noses grew longer; they lost control,
Thus, the end of all congressional leaders for whom the bells
now toll,
Fantasy yes, but quite understandable; quite picturesque, not
grotesque
And so the truth will out, as they check in at St. Peter's desk,
They have come to the end they most assuredly deserved,
For they forgot who they actually were elected to represent; who
they served
These Political Pinocchios, our "country's best," now laid to rest,
will have their day in court,
But not the one they envisioned, or sort.
I can hear them now, still playing the law maker-faker,
Forgetting that they are dealing now with their Maker
I'm sure they'll eternally roam their Creator's Lower Acre; their
actions never to recur,
And the media, their friends, will be overwhelmed, exhausted,
handling this

"THE CONGRESSIONAL MASSACRE"

"THE PRESENT"

A Gift?

To see the light of day is the greatest blessing of each morn,
It's the announcement of continued life, a new, joyous dawn,
We've been given more time, and a new slate,
A chance to change the world and our own fate,
Look to the future, each moment is precious, dear.
Each day that I live, I will always shout it loud and clear,

"REMEMBER!
NEVER LOOK AT THE PRESENT
FROM THE REAR"

I'M DREAMING …

DON'T STOP ME …

LIFE IS TOO SHORT!

"THEY SAY"

"They" say,
And the world they sway,
Those ever-living, ever-present phantoms of total control,
Living within the chasms of the mind; ever on patrol,
"They" say this; "they" say that,
"They" are trite; a thought automat.
When anyone lacks an answer yet wants to be heard,
"They say" thunders forth; right or wrong, it's absurd.
Who are these cretins of word and mind?
Who wander free and are with conversations intertwined?
"They say" doesn't impress me in the least
"They" are uncontrolled and untamed; each nothing but a
wildebeest
If "they," collectively, were reduced to a singular lot,
"They" would loose their power—eh, what?
If "they say" were changed to "I believe,"
I'd be ecstatic; I'd be relieved
I'd see a brighter tomorrow
There'd be more logic, more thought, more joy, less sorrow
To those who say "they say" often, here's a tip:
Loosen up; then, get a grip,
Unfasten your "they-sayers"
For often "they" are naysayers."
"They" close the lid on the box of imagination, free thought,
"They" try to direct and control all we have learned and have
been taught.

Forget their theory;

It makes me leery.

I'll express myself clearly, do what I do, think what I think, and

say what I say,

But never, no, never believe in or listen to what

"THEY SAY"

"THEY"

"Life is what you make it," so "they" say,
Who the hell are "they?"

I disagree—
My life is not mine to make it me.

My life belongs to those known as "they,"
Everyone else who had something to say,

Each one who lived, passed, and left a thought behind
Directed and affected my life, as defined.

My life is what I make it—that's incomprehensible—untrue.
It's a mosaic, colorful, many tidbits of every historian's chattel—
what "they" knew.

Although silenced by time and present state, "they" still have a say.
Collectively speaking, who are we, but

"THEY"

"OH, TO ROAM THE SKY AT NIGHT"

There it is for all to see,
Beckoning, beckoning, "Come to me, come to me,"
And, oh, how I would love to travel among the stars,
Convince a few to come home with me and fill my candy jars.
I'd have my own Tinkerbells to shine in the dark,
To keep me company, be my life's spark,
Twinkle me to sleep, when Mr. Sandman fails to show,
Tiny, bright, flickering lights, without a shadow,
And should you tire of me and my life, I will understand,
Release you to fly again, back to your homeland,
But do invite me to visit every now and again,
To dine, and enjoy your cloud soda fountain.
I can just imagine what a wonderful, unexpected treat,
Sugar cones and cotton candy … oh, how sweet,
And watching all those little cherubs swinging here and there,
Laughing and singing without a care.
How beautiful; what a lovely sight,
Peace and quiet, with melodies soft; what a delight,
But who would believe me, if I were to dare share this tale?
They'd tell me to bail: "You've had too much ale."
But should such a visit come true,
How blest I'd be, and thankful to each of you.
Such a wonderful thought, or is it a dream?
What was that blinding light, that golden beam?
Can you imagine my plight?
Keeping this secret, this fantastic voyage—

"OH, TO ROAM THE SKY AT NIGHT"

"NATURE'S JUST FULL OF SURPRISES"

The willows weep without tears, and all trees have a bark,
The wind whistles, and the air holds the trill of a lark,
Sunbeams caress the minutest of minute, and butterfly wings
flutter,
Owls hoot, birds chirp, and squirrels chatter; cows provide an utter,
I look and listen and stand in wonderment and awe,
The list is endless; why not add more, and more, and more, and
more?
Why stop there, when the count reaches a trillion and rises and
rises?
All that joy and more—

"NATURE'S JUST FULL OF SURPRISES"

"WHAT DID IT REALLY WANT TO SHARE?"

A bug buzzed me this morning, behind my ear.
I wonder what it was trying to share.
It didn't light, nor did it bite—
Thank you—
Simply whispered a little "Hello,"
And left me to wonder still,

"WHAT DID IT REALLY WANT TO SHARE?"

"'OFF' ON"

The bugs and stingers will always go for someone
who doesn't have their

"'OFF' ON!"

"BEAUTIFUL BUTTERFLIES"

Sometimes butterflies linger to let you enjoy their beauty and grace,
It's a though they feel safe as they look into your face,
They flutter and gently land on a bud or a flower,
Perhaps a leaf, or under the overhead, in a shower,
The ones of true majestic iridescent color are rare today,
They seem to have gone into permanent hibernation, out of our way,
For they know that nets and hands have taken too many for
their pleasure.
It's one thing to observe, and another to take life away for a
little treasure.
Now I ask you, how would you like to be captured and pinned
to a cushion?
The world would be a different place if only we could put
ourselves in that or another's position.
For the butterfly is so delicate, graceful, and pleasing to the eye,
Why can't we humans simply let it live to fly and fly and fly?
Abandon all the nets given to children; teach them to enjoy and
respect another's existence.
Taking away the life of something that has no defense is surely
an act of violence.
The butterfly in all its beauty is surely a prime example of grace,
Most often seeking a quiet, secure, and peaceful tiny dwelling
place,
So you see how close to humans they are in their desire.
If only we all could live in harmony, each the other to admire,
We might find peace in this world by looking deep into each
other's eyes,
Learn lessons so needed in one of God's most lovely creations,

"BEAUTIFUL BUTTERFLIES"

"GATHER IN THE GARDEN"

Is there always an auspicious beginning to spring?
Yes, because it has the toughest time to convert to dazzling,
After all, the earth is rock hard; it's now beginning to thaw,
Nature's roots are just awakening and have to find a door,
They rise slowly at first, then burst forth in silent song,
And the world looks on in wonder, and smiles as it walks along,
A bud here, a bud there—
And suddenly buds everywhere,
Each one, no doubt, anxious to rise from its long, cold slumber,
To spring forth with hues and colors too many to number,
Each one crying, "Look at me,
I'm the most beautiful in this season's land sea.
Rested we did in the heart of the earth,
Then slowly we set out to rise and share our worth,
Every single bud, every blossom, every flower in sight,
Thanking its Creator for life, warmth, and sunlight."
There's nothing less than glory, when spring has sprung—
Amen!
But it can only happen when we

"GATHER IN THE GARDEN"

"THE FIRE OF FALL"

The turning of the leaves,
The sun ablaze upon their deep rich yellows, oranges, cherry reds,
My heart grieves.
They're shouting, "Look at me," dancing with delight.
They're warmed by the sun, cooled by the breeze,
As they twist and turn on the whispers of the wind,
They're on their way out,
Dying with each twist and turn,
And that's the cause of my dismay.
They are leaving me,
Leaving me to sigh and sadly say,
"Stay, don't go; for I will miss the joy of your magnificent
splendor,
I will miss the crisp rustle of each leaf,
And, after you're gone, what will be left?"
The twisted black twigs of winter, covered with snow.
How quick the changes of the seasons!
Unfortunately, today, it's the passing of fall.
Swift, like the flickering flame, the dying ember,
These moments of joy will pass like last summer's thunder,
But somehow within my heart I know, no matter what the season,
The picture remains clear.
For some reason, I always remember

"THE FIRE OF FALL"

Silly me ...

"O, MY BRUSSELS SPROUT"

The brussels sprout forgot to grow,
For if it had, it'd be cabbage, ya know.
It looks the same—a mini version,
But the fork and knife have less excursion.
Tasty little devil—gassy too—
It probably grew in the same doo-doo.
Can't fool me; you're just another little kraut,
But I still love ya,

"O, MY BRUSSELS SPROUT"

"my little sweet pea"

So happy, round, and roly-poly—that's me!
My, my, it's crowded in here; I've got to get free.

I hear, to succeed, one must break loose from the pod,
Share the trappings given by God.

You're different than others who share your space.
Can't you tell by your thinking, and how others look at your
face?

Did you think that I meant break loose from my skin?
No, no, it's the thinking trapped within.

Reach for the top of the mountain; that's my philosophy—
Don't roll around on the ground,

"my little sweet pea"

"MY LOVELY LITTLE LEPRECHAUNS"

To all I say, "Join with us——tweak your twirly minds."

My little leapin' sprites,
Doin' fast and fancy jigs; now, that delights.
Singin' and chatterin', as only wee folk can
Their eyes are twinklin'; quick, put on a mischief ban
They can flit and fly faster than any flea.
That's why they can't be caught; they're too hard to see.
They'll not share their gold, but they'll bring a kettle of luck,
And if yer lucky enough, you'll see and enjoy their antics when
they go amok.
They can't sit still for a minute; sure, they're on the run
They don't want to be caught and bottled for someone else's fun
But should you be a-catchin' one of me little friends, please
note; they'll pretend to be dead,
For I know they'll surely do a number on yer head.
They're clever little creatures sent from above,
To honor St. Patrick, to bring pots of joy and love,
And, "Why are they so quick?" you might ask.
They have but twenty-four hours to fulfill their mighty task,
Then, my little green fleas, the wee folk, will be withdrawn,
And sleep again, each day, beyond tomorrow's dawn.
They have a year before comin' back with their mischief-filled
carry-ons,
So to them, I say, "Sleep well; I'll await your return,

"MY LOVELY LITTLE EPRECHAUNS"

63

"OH, TO BE A LEPRECHAUN"

Gosh, wouldn't it be fun to be a leprechaun?
To stuff a year's worth of mischief into one day, and then be gone?
Oh, that would be a lot of fun,
To scare the giants, make 'em run
Like elephants at the sight of mice—
Oh, now, wouldn't that be nice?
Behave yerself, you're beginnin' to become a wee-folk thinker.
Some might consider you then, none less than a stinker.
But then I'll remind them of me treasure,
That giant trove of happiness and pleasure,
Mischief has a place with the pot of gold and luck,
Therefore, I have every right to run amok.
Besides, it's only for 86,400 seconds; then I'd be gone,
To dream on—oh, the joy—

"OH, TO BE A LEPRECHAUN"

"LOST IN AN IRISH MIST"

Am I writing about a cordial drink?
Or, a fog? What do ye think?

I should be writing about the "Wearin' o' the Green,"
But I'm housebound today; the green's been unseen.

I haven't seen a fling or a jig,
I haven't had a libation—not even a swig,

I haven't heard an Irish ditty,
Or a joke from anyone particularly witty,

Ye see, this St. Patty's Day must silent remain,
Because it will go, just as it came,

Therefore, I'm writin' about the things in this list,
Which are unfortunately,

"LOST IN AN IRISH MIST"

"A MINI-SLEEP AT A TRAFFIC LIGHT"

I can't tell you how many times I have sat behind a "headless" driver.
I wish that all roads were at least two cars wider.
By God, move over, if you're going to snooze,
Or I'll call a cop and have you arrested for booze.
I'll lie; say you were weaving, dodging and driving crazy.
Are you truly that tired or just plain lazy?
Tell me now, before I lose my cool,
Before I make myself a complete fool,
When the light changes from red to green, time to go,
So hit the accelerator, you're not on your sofa, you know.
Move on, that's a car you're in, whether day or night,
Remember, you're not entitled to

"A MINI-SLEEP AT A TRAFFICE LIGHT"

"A SPEED LIMIT of THIRTY-FIVE MILES PER HOUR?"

Can you imagine what might happen if the speed limit was
dropped to thirty-five miles per hour?
We'd have half the road kill, and animals at roadside would no
longer cower.
Wouldn't it be delightful to be able to slow down?
I'd be ecstatic to walk, not run, around the town.
It would take twice as long to travel from place to place,
But there would be fewer accidents to trace.
We might even be able to carry on a civil conversation with ma
and pa,
A captive audience with a new mantra within their car,
But to be frank, I'm sure road rage would increase beyond
measure,
Because speedsters would not appreciate the new found
pleasure,
Ooo, I can just feel the sparks jump and fly
As cars rush for the lead position, noting, "I'm first, bye-bye."
Unfortunately, we live in a world of supersonic speed and man-
made power.
Do you think that we could ever return to

"A SPEED LIMIT of THIRTY-FIVE MILES PER HOUR?"

"WHY AN ITCH DESERVES A SCRATCH"

If for no other reason, its indefatigableness …
—Jeanette Dowdell

An itch is the most persistent irritant I know,
And if gently placated, it might just take a hike and go.
You can't zap an itch, like an annoying, buzzin' bug,
But you sure can answer back, with a scratch or a shrug.
The worst of all of these mighty devils is the one you can't reach,
Doorframes, backscratchers, sticks, don't satisfy the little
"beech."
I believe persistence, like the squeaky wheel, must be met head-
on,
With whatever means it takes, besides yelling, "Oh, be gone."
So, my little itch,
I give credit, you little witch,
For driving me crazy, making my skin crawl and twitch.
Have you ever felt the sting of a simple switch?
That would be the final blow,
For that would hurt me more, you know?
An ostrich I will not become,
And persistence renders you not dumb,
So let's negotiate, one "itch" to another.
For right now I have one word, one thought for you; it's
"smother."
I give you credit, but will not give in by admitting I've met my
match.
For what it's worth, I'll be tellin' the world just

"WHY AN ITCH DESERVES A SCRATCH"

"A DRIP?"

The obvious is a dumb individual,
But it could be a coffee percolator grind,
Or a drop of water, followed by another and another and
another;
Now that's one of the most interesting.
It could emanate from the faucet,
The garden hose,
The mouth.
A tear is usually referred to as a drop,
But it actually is a drip of salty water.
When is a drip a drop, and a drop, a drip?
Can a drip be a drip without being a drop?
Can a drop be a drop, without a being a drip?
Truly, what's the difference, between a drop and

"A DRIP?"

"DUST IS A MUST"

Otherwise, we wouldn't have people coming and going,
We wouldn't have people reaping and sowing,

We wouldn't have life and death; man's beginnings and end,
"Dust to dust"—descend and ascend,

"DUST IS A MUST"

"HOUSE DUST BUNNIES"

They hide in the craziest places,
Trying to fill hidden, yet open spaces,
Then, when they begin to feel crowded and tight,
They rush out of hiding into embarrassing sight.
Out in the open, they march and whirl;
On drafts and wind, they stir and swirl,
Crying silently, "Look at us, come on, look at us," their plea,
"Pick us up, so we can lie still, yet be free,
There's too much ground to cover bouncing about with ease,
We're not outdoor bunnies; we're only

"HOUSE DUST BUNNIES"

"SKELETONS IN THE CLOSET— YOURS, MINE, OURS, AND THEIRS"

Skeletons in the closet are always ready to pop out,
And when they do, they have quite a clout.
Everyone buries a skeleton from time to time,
A secret, best hidden in its present clime
What a juicy place that would be to visit,
Strange, but I think that I would enjoy it.
Could I live with myself having heard all that dirt?
Perhaps there would be some things about me that might hurt.
Of course, that depends upon which closet I might invade,
The group into which I will wade
Do you have any skeletons in your closets, my friends?
Perhaps some special family blends?
They don't take up much room, you know,
And when you move in, the prior skeletons should have left;
they should go,
No connection, no knowledge, the obvious reason
To leave one behind after you leave would be tantamount to
high treason.
There would be no reason for their existence; all the reasons
would be gone,
For all the creators would have moved on.
But some will be persistent, I'm sure.
They'll hide, wanting to stay and endure.
Each skeleton is a piece of one's conscience, heart, and mind.
They're usually placed in the closet to hide a hurt; to be kind,
But some are hidden for ammunition, to be used at a later date.
They're very patient; they have plenty of time to wait.

The closet with its secret store is not buried; it's above ground,
And all those little dandy devils just hang around.
They probably giggle and cavort when they sense release,
But shrivel in dismay when those moments are quelled,
disappear, cease.
Thwarted again … not brought out into the open,
Nary a hint … not even a token,
Too many secrets go to the grave with their owners, they do,
And the skeletons go with them; out of the closet, they're through.
Skeletons are so alive when hidden behind closed doors,
But they are put away complete with all their spiritual flaws.
They never have a say in the matter, unless the owners fess up.
Then they can face a full-blown flare, or a simple hiccup.
That depends upon how serious a matter they represent; who
they are,
One that tweaks, or one that can totally jar
Be it known, they have, I believe, a pecking order in their space;
The most serious cases hold a much higher place.
When they are released, things are never the same—
Lives change, agendas die, much goes up in flame.
They are a powerful lot.
They control many a day and situation; weak they are not,
And knowledge of their existence causes hidden distress; it wears.
But don't fret; just remember who they are …

"SKELETONS IN THE CLOSET— YOURS, MINE, OURS, AND THEIRS"

"LET ME OUT!"

I'm a memory, trapped without air, light, or food,
I've become a skeleton in this family's closet

Let me out!
Let me fly through the air
And laugh at other's reactions to my freedom,
Quelling their thoughts, whispers, gossip, and rumors

Let me out!
So I can scrape the crust off their pettiness, their bones,
Destroy their ever-searching troublemaking minuscule gossip-
mongering minds
And fill the space with something worthwhile

Let me out!
So that no one ever again will have to worry about my
accidental escape
And all its ramifications,
For the longer I am encapsulated, the more the dust will fly
when I am released

Let me out!
My freedom represents your freedom;
You'll be free to do, say, and act as you want,
For the heavy burden of deceit will be released

Let me out!
Take on a new life perspective.
There will be no future surprises,

No negative explosions,
No more worrying about me, your hidden skeleton

So I leave you with something to think about,
I leave you with some sound advice,

"LET ME OUT!"

More Words ...

"I DINE ON RHYME"

I think in rhyme.
Deep down and personal, it's mine,
A veritable feast of words that interlock,
Ready to swing into action like the endless ticking clock,
What says it best; what fits?
The plate is full—challenging my wits,
It's like selecting my favorite foods with delight.
I'll search 'til I find the absolute word—the one that's just right.
Rarely, if ever, do I go hungry at any time,
Whether on Earth, or in a higher clime—

"I DINE ON RHYME"

"WORDS, WORDS, WORDS"

They lead, they guide, they taunt, they fire imagination, they
direct, they train, they mesmerize, they entertain, they live,
they die, they describe, they instruct, they torment, they tell,
they inform, they employ, they educate, they enrich our lives
without measure, they are the means of communication, they
enthrall, they are a celebration of life, they irritate, they soothe,
they sell, they bless, they explain,
No matter what the language—body or spoken—they are what
they are …
And what would we all be without them?

"WORDS, WORDS, WORDS"

"RIGOR MORTIS OF THE LIVING BRAIN"

Why not? You're creative juices are dying at the door. "Knock,
knock,"
Nothing's happening; some call it writer's Block,
Not a bad thought, because the brain feels dead,
You can't think of any bright quote, anything recently said,
It's as if your brain has turned to stone,
It's a wee pea, the smallest—actually, one never grown,
Words flow, but sentences fail to form,
Certainly not cricket; definitely not norm
So you talk to yourself, ask self for an awakening word or two,
Otherwise, you just don't know what you'll do,
Go ahead, whack your head hard; jar something loose,
Look around; take it in—nature, life, moose, and goose,
Perhaps a song, a haunting melody—ah, a simple tune, a
beautiful refrain,
Well, if nothing comes, you're stuck; diagnosis, definitely,

"RIGOR MORTIS OF THE LIVING BRAIN"

"WE'RE ONLY ON LOAN"

The question often arises, why must we die?
Most feel we return to the sky,
As if we know from whence we came,
And that our Creator will someday our souls reclaim.
Our spirits are plucked from their earthly home on cue,
And they, without direction, seem to know exactly what to do.
Without question, we'd all like more time to share,
To do some things we always wanted to, but didn't dare,
But we're not in charge of our time on Earth.
That was more than likely determined at birth.
And time, at times, moves much too fast,
Particularly when we want certain moments to last
But what is a moment in today's technologically communicative
world?
In bygone days, it would take days or weeks to be unfurled.
Borrowed time is what our lives are all about,
But borrowed from what, and where—space, no doubt.
As the mind settles on more mature thought, one conclusion
can be drawn—one alone.
Conception is the beginning of a time-sensitive contract; yes—

"WE'RE ONLY ON LOAN"

"MOM, 'YOU ARE MY SUNSHINE"

Written for my friend Dorothy Welenc's mother, who suffered from dementia for twelve years before passing on January 31, 2005

"'You Are My Sunshine,' my only sunshine,"
A song of love
For one whom long ago left time behind,
And is unaware of her twilight zone,
She no longer knows whether it's morning or night,
Nor does she care,

For her mind remains in the midnight of life without a thought,
She no longer knows who holds her hand, but the holder feels
she does.
She no longer understands the functions of her body.
She groans and smiles, and unbeknownst to her, still shares the
twinkle in her eyes.

For her, life has given itself to another path; it's traveling
Alzheimer's Way,
Which not only takes the body, mind, and soul of its prey, but
all who care,
Can it be wrong to pray that her Creator bless her now,
With a kinder, gentler existence at His side?
Would we be praying for ourselves and the pain that grips us so?
Or for the soul of the mind, which is no longer able to live?

As only you can, God,
Please, give a precious moment of light,
A precious moment of joy,
A precious moment
For her to hear her daughter sing,

MOM, "YOU ARE MY SUNSHINE"

"AN EMPTY CHAIR"

An empty chair stares back at me.
How many ghosts of the past do I see?
I can name any number at my age,
Each played a part on my life's stage,
Now they're at rest, but with them special memories I share,
As I gaze in solitude at

"AN EMPTY CHAIR"

"THE SILENT GUITAR"

In Memoriam: "Uncle Jack" (John C. Barton), March 28, 1961

His guitar is silent now; he'll strum on Earth no more.
He has passed through God's musician's door.
His fingers, strong and powerfully fine,
Strummed his favorite tune and mine,
We would sit and listen and sing along
As his fingers played song after song after song,
That guitar stands lonely and silent in a corner now,
Weeping in a reverent bow,
It knows its master has passed away,
But it will not be silent for very long; just for this transition day.

"STICKBALL, PLUS"
Brooklyn, NY – Circa 1940's

Smell the summer heat,
On a good old city street
Taste a chunk of ice
Stolen off the ice truck on it rounds; how nice.
Feel the softness of the skin of a pink Spalding ball,
Smell its newness before it hits the pavement or a wall.
If it didn't have the familiar name painted on its skin,
We would yell forgery for sure, with a grin.
Check it out; it had to bounce higher than any other ball,
If not, it definitely was a fake; you call that ball a ball?
Okay, we're ready to play.
"Check out the sewer caps," someone would say.
Do we have enough bases?
Where are first and third? Identify their places,
"Here's first, the back fender of the black car."
"How about the Dodge for third; no, it's too far from second,
too far,
It's also too close to home; how about the tree trunk, or
telephone pole?"
Now, all that was the easy part; who is going to be on whose
team?
All voices were raised to a level of scream,
"Once, twice, three, shoot," and the fingers would appear,
Round, after round, 'til we had two teams, and a cheer
I never thought about it until now:
You only had one shot to win if you called odds—holy cow!
If you called evens, your chances were based upon two to win,

But with odds just one, kinda thin
Now we're ready to play; check out the bat.
All the old broom handles rolled out—short, long, skinny, and
fat.
Everyone had their favorites, no doubt,
The one that would kill the ball as it was batted about,
There was always a reminder before each game; "If you break a
window, don't forget to run, scatter,"
All the neighbors knew who we were, so what did it matter?
There was no place to hide
Except to run for a hallway and wait inside.
I was always on somebody's team,
I could hit the ball three sewers; that was keen.
No less than a double, usually a home run.
Oh, what fun; what fun!
Back then, the summer heat didn't mean a thing
As long as we were in a groove on our best swing,
Then, run like gazelles across the street kid's macadam field,
And, once the game began, the arguments went on forever; no
one would yield.
"He's out; he didn't touch first."
Everyone was an umpire; that was the worst.
I loved to run; the breeze made me cool,
Like jumping into the three foot pool,
The park wasn't that far away,
But stickball on the street; that was the way of the day,
We'd play until we lost the ball, or were called to go home
How boring; in those days, we had no television or a telephone.
It was a break for the neighbors, though, who were praying for
quiet and peace,
They could relax now, their tensions release.

I can still feel that summer heat,
The tar roadbed actually burned the soles of the feet.
Maybe that's why we kept running, to avoid sticking to the
ground.
Yes, there were spots we left imprints as the bases we'd round,
And when we'd loose the Spalding ball that was death for us,
Obviously, the memories live on; I can still feel the emotion of
the game—that crazy

"STICKBALL, PLUS"

"BIRDS IN FLIGHT"

I'd love to be a part of the conversations of a flock of birds in flight,
After their rest, during their early morning journey coming out
of night
Do they feel the sunrise on their feathers and in their bones?
Are they squawking words, or are their sounds old birds' groans?
I wonder how they choose their leader—maybe by raising a wing—
The one who guides them on their journey into next spring
Look into their eyes—you can see them think.
They talk, but have you ever seen them wink?
I love to watch them float and glide
With the same rhythm as the ebb and flow of a soft tide,
They kiss the air just as water busses the sand.
They love the sky, as we love the land.
I'd like to hitch a ride as they swoop and dive with all their might.
However, I'm satisfied; I've been blessed with a wonderful gift,
just to see

"BIRDS IN FLIGHT"

"GROW ME FEET!"

Don't you think that those who cannot walk, those who have
no legs or feet,
don't cry out in their wilderness to a power far beyond their
comprehension, and scream,

"Grow Me Feet!"

Don't you think that they want to walk with those who walk,
run with those who run, jump with those who jump, hop, skip,
etc.?

Don't you think that those who cannot see don't cry out from
their darkness to ask—no, beg—for the light of day to brighten
their world?

"Grow Me Sight!"

Don't you think that they want to see, enjoy, and reap all the
benefits of everything there is in the realm of Creation?

Don't you think that those who have no arms and hands reach
out in vain in mental anguish to grasp a miracle beyond their
reach, while not losing hope and quietly whispering,

"Grow Me Hands!"

Don't you think that they long to return a hug or hold a hand
to comfort someone in need?

Don't you think that all who are different, deformed, and disabled would like to look into the eyes of those who look at them and see the same gaze given others who are whole, not challenged?

"Grow Me Acceptance!"

Don't you think that we all know in a glance what others are seeing and feeling, whether there is acceptance and compassion, without the gaze of pity that accompanies our greeting?

"Grow Me Understanding!"

Don't you think that we all are strong enough to develop a level of acceptance that overshadows our inability to show our obvious deep sense of pity?

"Grow Me Perspicacious Subliminal Compassion!"

"GROW ME FEET!"

"GIMME FIVE"

Dedicated to "Dusty," September 9, 2009, Ruth Overton's
Brittany Spaniel
When he heard the words "Gimme five," he'd sit and give you
his paw.

"Gimme five" is gone,
Restored and roaming the Great Beyond,
Playing and resting in Doggie Heaven above,
Knowing he had many years filled with deep love.
From day one, his beautiful brown eyes gazed into mine.
We bonded, became friends for all time.
Time for you to have full days of fun with others of your kind,
Friends to romp with, treats to find,
I'm sure you'll find Toto and Hagar, your walkin' buddies,
With no need to fight any of Earth's irritating "buggies,"
Fleet of paw, you'll chase the squirrels up a tree,
Goin' at will on a wild runnin' and jumpin' spree,
Looking down through the same warm eyes we shared, me and you,
And I will hold them in my memory until my time is through.
I loved when you visited at my back door
And waited in anticipation for a treat or two or more,
But somehow, you never really got beyond two.
Your mommy would always say, "That's enough today for you."
It was just my way of saying I loved you very much;
Therefore, I know, we'll always keep in touch,
And now I can tell you, my friend, I appreciated your smile.
It was as though you turned your love up a notch on your
doggie dial.
True, life moves on, as it must,

But you'll never be further away than my memory, I trust,
And when I want to feel your spirit come alive,
I'll just say, "Hey, Dusty,

GIMME FIVE!"

"BECAUSE OF YOU"

In Loving Memory
SAMANTHA CALI, "THE CAT"—April 10, 1999–March 4, 2009

Because of you
The sky was more blue,
Butterfly wings had a more vivid hue,
The sun and moon were brighter,
And my heart was always much lighter.

Because of you,
Life's trials seemed less intense,
Everything made perfect sense,
For love always shone bright in your eyes,
And when there was a need, you came close—warm and wise.

Because of you,
Long days were shorter,
You were my friend—a generous and faithful supporter,
You had to move on, yet you'll ever be near,
You were a treasure, most valued and dear.

Because of you,
My heart is fuller, you see,
You'll rest within forever, a special memory.
I know God is holding you in His arms, already made you
whole and new,
For He knows you deserve the best, my pet; He knows you.

Because of you,
My life was truly blessed.
Embrace we will, come my day of rest.
I've lived ten years with unconditional love, undeniably true,
Yes, my love, all

"BECAUSE OF YOU"

God Bless

"WAITIN' AT THE GATE"

I wonder who will be waitin' at the Gate—
Besides Saint Peter, who will deliver my fate?
The biggest shock would be if no one was there.
Would it mean that no one really did care?
That would be like having no mother to deliver me at birth,
When I first arrived, landed on Earth,
If I had my druthers, I know who I would want to be there,
But would they want to be at the gate; would they care?
I'd put my pets at the front of the line,
They wouldn't have to think it over; their loyalty will still be mine,
I want instant hugs, licks, and kisses, their love of old,
And forgiveness for the many times I did punish and scold,
Next would be my closest family and friends,
For me, this will be the time their passing away ends,
I have no doubt that there will be laughter mingled with tears,
Lost warmth and love and joy will replace their resting years,
If I have my way, they'll be a crowd at The Gate,
For reunions can never come too late.
Of course, not everyone can be first; some will have to wait a
little longer.
Perhaps their love was lesser, rather than stronger,
And, obviously, those I do not desire to meet at all will have the
longest wait.
Love will be the key; define the order, and who I want to be

"WAITIN' AT THE GATE"

93

"TIME, TICK, TIME, TOCK, TIME, TICK, TIME, TOCK, TIME ..."

I haven't written about time in a long time.
I think it's time,
But right now, it's 2:15 a.m.
I really don't have time.
Tomorrow, I will take time,
If life gives me time.
Isn't this dream time?
Doesn't it belong to someone else?
I always hear my meter running.
Is it running down?
I wonder how long it will be before
I run out of time
And
Will I find that I will always have time?
Check the time, the clock—
Is it ticking?
If not, plug it in
Or get a new battery.
Never fall behind time.
You may never catch up with that lost time.
Wasted time is gone forever.
The clock is metering out your time,
And my time,
Listen,

"TIME, TICK, TIME, TOCK, TIME, TICK, TIME, TOCK, TIME ..."

"THERE AIN'T NO STORAGE
IN THE GREAT BEYOND"

If I can't whistle on my way to heaven, I'll know I'm on my way
to hell,
I just gotta take my whistle; otherwise, I'll be sick, not well.
Not only is my whistle my trademark of note,
It's light as a feather, easy to tote.
Besides, if the buzzer is broken at the Pearly Gate,
I can whistle while I wait.
I'd never run out of songs.
Just don't count them as my wrongs.
I certainly wouldn't call St. Peter like callin' a cab,
For surely I'd hit the slippery slope with nothin' to grab,
But that's not the point, you see,
I don't know how long this journey will be,
And my whistle will be a comfort along the way,
It might even attract others I knew in another day,
I wonder what St. Peter would think if I arrived at his gate with
a crowd?
Announcing, "I'm here, I hope I'm not too loud.
I didn't bring any earthly possessions, except my whistle,
No excess, no furniture, no toys, no crystal,
After all, my whistle is air, like my spirit as I travel on,
And believe me, St. Peter, I've been told

THERE AIN'T NO STORAGE IN
THE GREAT BEYOND!"

"SORROW SO DEEP"

DEDICATED TO THIS LAND'S OWNERS OF OLD—
THE AMERICAN INDIANS
Kenny Smith's vision, which I, too, saw quite vividly

I see them standing among the trees,
Watching cars and trucks roll by.
Their tears flow,
And so do mine.
I can read the look upon their faces,
See the hurt in their eyes,
Feel their sorrow,
Read their minds.
"Where has our homeland gone?
Where are the forests of life?
Our legacy,
Our country, so pure, and clean, and fresh"
Their tears flow,
And so do mine.
I feel their heartache, their bitterness,
Suffer with them their great sense of loss,
Their hopelessness, their powerlessness,
Their inability down through the ages to stop this terrible
plight,
Stop the destroying of trees—homes for all the animals they
loved so dear,
Why, God?
For the building of huge homes—monuments to gluttony and
greed?

For the building of roads and shopping malls—a new way of
life?
Yes, they stand tall,
Straight as the arrows they shot from their bows.
They stare,
In silent grief, they stare.
As they stand among the trees and observe progress in motion,
Their tears flow,
And so do mine:

"SORROW SO DEEP"

"NATURE—NOW EXTINCT"

Whispering reeds,
Babbling brooks,
Breezes searching company,
Tides on their ebb and flow,
Chirping birds and chattering squirrels,
Hoot owls hooting,
Rustling leaves and falling acorns,
All the fragrances of the seasons,
Gone!
Replaced by exhaust, motor noise,
Man's creations,
What have we done?

"WHO TAUGHT THE TREE?"

Who taught the tree how to grow?
Who taught its branches to sprout leaves?
To grow up, out, droop, or hug a limb
To quench its thirst and share its store,
To sway in the dry old wind and not crack into two or more parts,
To give up dry old branches, which steal life from new growth?
Who taught the buds to bud, when to grow, change colors, and
fall away on cue?
Who is responsible for such deeds?
Could it be just a happening?

"WHO TAUGHT THE TREE?"

"I WANNA KNOW—WHO?"

Who taught a baby to breathe?
Who supplied the air?
Who taught the fish to swim, the bird to fly and sing, and
the bee to buzz?
Who told the rock to be as hard as it is?
Who taught the water to flow and be wet?
Who taught the rain and snow to form and fall?
Who taught my eyes to see, and my mouth to speak?
Who gave the pine and spruce their needles?
Who shaped the leaves of the oak, the maples, and the birch?
Who told the weeping willow to weep and move with the grace
of angels?
Who taught the dog to bark, the cow to moo, the cat to meow,
and the horse to whinny?
Oh, pooh,
Who gave the bunny rabbit its big ears, fluffy white tail, and
not me?
Who taught the snakes to slither and the kangaroo to hop?
Who taught the nails to grow, and how, on each defined
appropriate digit?
Who taught the owl to hoot, the crow to caw, and the canary to
sing?
Who made eyes to blink and tear and communicate?
Who taught the brain to function as it does, to make all the
other intricate parts work?
Oh, pooh,
Who did all of this, plus, plus, plus, et cetera?

"I WANNA KNOW—WHO?"

"WHEN WILL ENOUGH
EVER BE ENOUGH?"

Unfortunately, our lives are based on *more:*
The more we have, the more we want.
When did we, as a society, change our thinking from *need* to *want?*
I can't remember when the transition first took place,
Can you?
Was it after World War II
Or did it begin in the 1950s and 60s?
How about the 1970s and 80s?
Was the potential for its birth and propagation always there?
Or did it emerge as a result of financial improvements and
credit becoming acceptable and rampant?
In prior decades—centuries—only the wealthy could be
extravagant,
It seems to me that everyone else was simply making ends meet,
Today, almost everyone in America lives beyond their means;
Almost everyone lives in the world of satisfying wants, not need,
I want a house, I want a bigger house, I want two houses,
I want two cars, I want filet mignon.
Whatever happened to public transportation, a place to live that
was just big enough for the family's needs?
Whatever happened to franks and beans and a hamburger or stew?
We all have somehow changed our *wants* into *needs,* and
justified the behavior,
Not only have we created this accepted way of life, we
knowingly insist on its perpetuation.
Isn't the skin of this growing bubble getting thinner with each
successive generation—

in fact, with each minute?
I wonder if anyone today knows or can define the difference
between what they *need,* and what they *want,*
And I wonder, too, if the answer would be material or non-
material?
Today, our voices echo in surrounding empty space.
Who is the richer for fostering greater debt, more "must haves,"
larger and larger edifices in which to live?
Am I?
Are you?
Are we?
Tell me, if you can,

"WHEN WILL ENOUGH
EVER BE ENOUGH?"

"GREED"

Like those pesky garden weeds,
Which grow faster than our cultivated seeds,
There are those who dwell among us of a certain ilk and misdeed.
They live their lives exhibiting but one basic principle—greed.
When they succeed and it works for them, why change?
Wouldn't that be unusual; wouldn't that be strange?

Holiday Thoughts ...

"IT'S OVER"

GOOD-BYE

The hoopla, the hollering, the horns, the bells,
With the old year we've shared our fond farewells,
Sometimes I think we are reliving a ritual of ancient days,
One to ward off spirits with evil ways,
My taste leans more toward a quiet supper with family and close friends,
An "Auld Lang Syne" with a bit of bubbly when the old year ends,
For as long as I can remember, I've disliked New Year's Eve celebrations.
I view them for what they are, forced orchestrations:
Balloons, confetti, noise, and booze,
Everyone trying desperately their inhibitions to lose,
It just doesn't make sense; I'm sure the New Year will agree.
It has become a worldwide epidemic with a human cry, "Go ahead try to outdo me."
Who cares? The New Year will have its way—not all clover,
As for the old year, without a doubt, it's gone ...

"IT'S OVER"

"MAKE A DIFFERENCE"

I'm conscious of my conscience,
Now, if only my conscience would be more conscious of me.
Who's in charge here, anyway?
It's a new year,
And I'll be as conscious of my conscience as I can be.
That's fair, isn't it?
What do you expect me to be, an angel?
It's resolution time,
I'll make some, but with a difference this year,
With a vow to keep the resolutions I make,
I'm determined, I'm determined, I'm determined!
Conscience speaking: "No, you're not!"
"I will, I will!"
Conscience speaking: "No you won't."
"We'll see."
Conscience speaking: "Resolutions most always are broken;
they're too self-centered,
But what if they went beyond self?
Wouldn't they be more demanding; more worthwhile?"
"What do you expect me to be, an angel?"
Conscience speaking: "Yes!
More patient, kind, considerate, loving, aware,
Give others hope,
Help someone else's aspirations and dreams come true,
Nourish souls, feed the hungry, and dry the tears of those who cry,
Make laughter ring, and support the faint of heart,
Give your youthful spirit to those who watch endless time tick.
You can do it,
And then I'll believe that you are determined!

Think in God's terms,
And remember, there are angels, and there are angels,
Then, there's you and me,
Let's make a resolution we can keep,
Be an angel:

"MAKE A DIFFERENCE"

"LEAPERS"

For a special friend WVF

Only once every four years this type of year will surface.
It's called Leap Year, and it has a definite purpose.
Without it, our calendars would not jive.
We must add a day, each four years for it to survive.

Leapers, as those born on this day are called, lose out in many
ways,
Unless of course, they share other people's birthdays,
The usual denoted day of celebration each non-leap year is
February 28th,
The normal last day of the month; but it's not their zenith.
And isn't that sad, not to have a birthday of your own
each year?
That's why, and I understand, the louder they must cheer,
"It's my day; mine and other Leapers too!"
It's special, and Leapers are too, because they number so few.
On average, only 1,461 babies are born on this day every four
years ... exact to the date.
So, never forget that they are amazing, and they should always
rate.
Plus, please note, one of the strongest men in history was given
this honor too.
He's known worldwide as Superman to me and you.
They're not different; they just give us a reason to be weepers.
After all, we have to add four years to every one they celebrate,
because they're

"LEAPERS"

"HAPPY ST. PATRICK'S DAY"

ME LITTLE LEPRECHAUN and ME

I woke up this mornin' to see a leprechaun laughin' at me,

He was sittin' bold as ye please, on the alarm clock, ye see.

He was in a dauntless and tauntin' mood, definitely,

But I knew I would have the last laugh so I did a quiet tee-hee,

All I had to do was wait for the alarm to ring,

And so it did, and with a shock and a big surprise, he did a flying fling.

He flew through the air squealin' all the way,

But, that won't be the end of it for me today.

He'll be back with his mischief totin' mind in high gear,

So I'll be a-watchin' me steps, and waitin'—oh, dear, oh dear.

Ye never know what the wee folk might have up their sleeve— today's giant wish,

Their special jovial tidbits waitin' to be released, while in a state quite "peevish."

I'm sure he is upset that I didn't say scat, or shoo him off my clock

Before the alarm sent him reelin' and put 'im in shock.

No doubt now, for him I'm a big piece of leprechaun bait,

He's a-waitin' his turn; he's got plenty of time … he'll wait.

Then he'll wish me in his own inimitable way,

A very special, memorable

"HAPPY ST. PATRICK'S DAY"

"THERE'S NEVER A NEED TO FRET, HIS EASTER PROMISE IS HERE TO STAY"

EASTER

How bright! How beautiful!
How lovely! How grand!
But only for those who truly have faith; those who truly believe,
understand.

Those on the fringe or in total denial of His Plan
Don't have the same strength on which to stand.

They leave to chance the many intricate wonders, the beauty of
the earth.
They don't have tomorrow's "after death" promise, so how can
they recognize its value, its worth?

No matter what it is you believe The Promise to be,
The faithful know earthly trials, tribulations, trauma will be no
more; they'll flee.

All they have to do is ask forgiveness, change their ways,
And their souls will find their promised rest in their everlasting
eternal days.

So I question those who refuse to recognize a Creator Divine.
Do all God's creations, some still unknown, fail with their
Creator to intertwine?

Do we still fail to realize that we'll never rise to God's creative genius; we're no match.
We can't stand alone; we're like floss, twisted threads of thread, unable to unlatch.

Families and corporations survive very often on some *tour de force,*
But I know of none who have lasted centuries, like Christ's Cross.

Some dismiss God, then ask, "What about tomorrow?" Ask the faithful; they know the way;
Their Jesus paved the path, and

"THERE'S NEVER A NEED TO FRET, HIS EASTER PROMISE IS HERE TO STAY"

"A HUG"

ANOTHER BLESSING FROM ABOVE

Our first hug is a temporary good-bye,
As we leave our home in the eternal sky,
When God caresses our soul and places it in the care of another,
To be warm and snug and nurtured inside the one you'll love
and call mother,
And for a very short time, you'll be hugged twenty-four hours a day,
Then, gently coaxed—nudged to join the world—be on your way,
Hugged by your mother's arms, held in quiet peace,
Until, of course, you scream, ask, no, plead, for release.
Year in and year out, the hugs gain greater meaning.
Later, your memory will recall and reel out that love you were
gleaning:
Hugs to keep you warm, heal a hurt, say thank you, or
recognize a job well done,
Those hugs reserved for special people, special occasions—hugs
for one,
How quickly we learn the one with the greatest hug store is a
mother,
The one who innately anticipates, without being prodded, the
needs of another,
The one who has mastered the art of sharing love,

The one who has been blessed with grace by angels above,
The one who understands without question the desperation in a
simple tug,
And knows the true meaning in giving and receiving

"A HUG"

HAPPY MOTHER'S DAY

"THEY DIED, SO WE COULD LIVE"

They died, so we could live,
They gave their most precious possession; what do we give?
Veterans, warriors, angels of a heavenly army, one and all, living and gone,
Deserve our best blessings and thanks and well beyond.
We cannot know the sorrow of such a loss,
As our youth, our strength, our heroes of history we always seem to toss.
For those who survived, a lifetime of mental and physical distress,
Living over and over the horrors of each circumstance they had to address.
Most living veterans lock away their wartime memories; they're, sacrosanct—theirs to hold,
Deep personal moments, not idle chatter to be shared or told,
With a few braggadocio exceptions who want the world to know about their many a mighty feat.
But most are grateful for having survived; respect the memory of their buddies, whose lives were never complete.
Those who gave all they had—their tomorrows—
So that someone else might live their time, the time that someone else now borrows,
Life, no matter how it's played, is always worth living,
To give it away to someone else is the ultimate in giving,
And when a veteran comes home from war, he has given something we never give,
A piece of his life, irreplaceable time, and it carries with it a new perspective.

They became part of a history written for all to see,
But the most blessed part is what they all left for you and me,
Praise be to each, forever, for what they did give,
Particularly those who paid the ultimate price—

"THEY DIED, SO WE COULD LIVE"

"MY FLAG"

I know where you are,
Standing tall in weightless wonder, awe and beauty,
Resting unattended in the silent heavenly reverence you deserve,
Protected.
Oh, my most precious and valuable symbol of freedom,
I see you clearly, not with my eyes, but my mind,
My dreams, and those of my country, put you there,
You are bathed in moonbeams,
Cradled in the hands of God,
Surrounded by the warm souls who fought so valiantly for, and
with you,
Those who gave their lives so others could live free,
I'm glad you are where you are,
Living in peace and serenity,
Out of harm's way,
Out of the reach of those who wish to destroy you,
A home away from home,
But one that affords you the greatest respect,
And therein lies hope…
I lift mine eyes;
My heart, my soul, my love, my life, and my eternal gratitude
are yours.
I look up to you with joy, oh, most blessed,

"MY FLAG"

"OH, MY MENORAH MINE"

THE MIRACLE—FESTIVAL OF LIGHTS

I remember the story well,
So much to glean, so much to tell,
The year was 165 BC.
Long-suffering Jews in Judea defeated Antiochus IV, thanks to
Judah Maccabee,
And in Jerusalem, he purged the Temple and replaced the
desecrated altar,
In that land so far away, in that land of suppression, filled with
spiritual hunger,
The Temple was rededicated to God with festivities that lasted
eight days,
Once again we found religious freedom to practice in our ways,
But after the battle, a problem arose; only one cruse of pure
olive oil was found,
Too little for a formal rededication in that moment so rare and
profound,
But somehow, miraculously, that's how long the oil burned,
History was forever rewritten, as we learned,
And in that time there was a famous Talmudic debate: "In
which order should the Hanukkah candles be lit?"
Two schools of thought were expressed, but only one was
granted a writ,
The School of Shamai claimed all eight lights should be set
ablaze at once, then reduced by one each night,
The School of Hillel, however, argued, to increase the holiness
in the world, the lights should be lit one each night to increase
the light,

We know which school of thought was taken to heart:
Even today, the Hanukkah candles on each candelabrum do their part,
The shamash, the servant, the ninth and smallest candle, will light each candle in turn,
Candles are lit from left to right to honor the newer thing first; that we learn,
But, as with all traditions, celebrations take on new tones,
However, like all true believers, our faith and holiness stays strong within our bones.
Today's celebration includes latkes, deep fried jelly donuts (Israel), gifts, dreidels, gelt, and songs with familiar tunes; for children of all ages, a happy sound,
"The dreidel on the floor goes round and round,"
"I'm a Little Teapot," "Little Latke,"
"Hanukkah Candles," "Ten Little Indians," in any key.
During Chanukah, gifts are exchanged, contributions given to the poor,
Happiness abounds for sure.
But in the end, what stands firm is faith and the knowledge of the miracle of light,
To brighten our darkest days, the times of deepest night,
And so the candles one by one are lit to let faith shine,
Keeping the symbol of the miracle ever bright, during and after, each celebration … 'til we meet again

"OH, MY MENORAH MINE
"HAPPY CHANUKAH"

MERRY CHRISTMAS

The star never shone brighter, to spread its meaning clearer. But how does one wrap and unwrap love?
—Jeanette Dowdell

"A CHRISTMAS FANTASY"

The Journey—The Christmas Visit

The children had named the horse, "Christmas," in honor of
their favorite holiday.
He was already hitched to our sleigh,
It had snowed, which made it perfect for Christmas Eve,
The night air was crisp, cool and clear when we were ready to leave,
A family visit awaited, replete with dear friends,
We didn't have far to go; just down the winding road to where
it ends,
We were dressed in our holiday best—no complaints,
Christmas would be gone before we blinked, and we'd wonder,
as always, where it went,
So we climbed into our sleigh with great anticipation,
We huddled to keep warm; sang some Christmas carols of
adoration,
Our canvas duffel bag filled with well-chosen gifts was covered
in case it should snow,
For each gift was special, wrapped and labeled just so;
Christmas led the way,
Sleigh bells jingling in cadence as he galloped in sway,
All was beautiful; stars twinkled and shone bright,

We knew it was going to be a warm and wonderful night,
Then suddenly without warning, one star brightened the sky,
It engulfed our sleigh, and soft melodic tinkling notes began to multiply,
Something strange was happening, to be sure,
Yet we remained calm—felt quite secure,
Our horse turned into a donkey; the carriage slowed in pace,
We were no longer traveling in today's hectic race,
Time seemed to stand still,
The star became brighter still as it hovered above the hill,
No one moved; there was enchantment all around,
Something filled the air, something special; would it astound?
The cover flew off the gift bag; the gifts gracefully floated away into the night,
Yet the bag remained full, bathed in starlight,
Aurora lights streamed from it; they were beyond inviting,
Whatever was happening was no less than exciting,
We all gathered round to take a peek,
Whatever was there did all but speak,
The scene took our breath away:
There was a father, and a mother holding a baby, with animals at bay,
There was no question about what we were seeing,
A very special birth; a very special tiny being,
Born to us on this night,
In light, brighter than light,
How privileged we were to share this moment in time, this re-visitation,
We bowed our heads in deep collective meditation,
What did this all mean? Who would ever believe?
Whoever did this night preconceive?
The light and scene began to dim,

The packages returned; they were now within,
However, each label had an additional notation,
There was a definitive mark for self-reflection,
The true meaning of the night, this life, was ablaze,
It would remain with us throughout our days,
For the packages now read for all to see,
Heartfelt messages—with love, compassion, concern, warmth,
peace, belief, joy, understanding, caring, friendliness, sincerity
And as we read, the tears began to flow,
The true meaning of Christmas has been returned; oh, how, we
now know,
The pace of our horse returned to norm,
And we were not only blessed forever, but so much more warm,
Inside and out, our lives had more meaning; we'd never be the
same,
We would live life differently, with new purpose and aim,
The hand of God reached down to caress our souls, open our
hearts,
Our lives were reborn, given a new start,
Yes, we enjoyed our holiday visit, without a doubt,
We were taken back in time to witness again what Christmas is
all about.
We'll celebrate forever, reliving that moment in faith-filled ecstasy,
For we reunited with the true meaning of Christmas in

"A CHRISTMAS FANTASY"

"SWEET DOVES OF PEACE"

Sweet Doves of Peace fly o'er fields of white crosses,
Counting once again all great nations' losses,
Fertile young lives snuffed out like a candle flame—
Who harbors the reason, and whom do we blame?

Sweet Doves of Peace flying in morn's early chill
Disturb the shadowy mist, the air so still,
O'er sanctums where freedom's defenders now rest,
Bathed in warm ethereal beams—heroes blessed!

Sweet Doves of Peace fly into a noon-high sun,
Asking, "When will this battle be won?
"How many more must die for their brother's sake?
"How many more must bear the pain and heartbreak?"

Sweet Doves of Peace fly in twilight silhouette,
Sensing every nation's tension and regret.
Each has given much for the world's future state.
Was it worth the effort? Is it worth the wait?

Sweet Doves of Peace flying o'er all nations,
War is not the destiny of God's creations!
By wisdom and patience humankind will survive,
By love and faith, freedom will be kept alive.

Sweet Doves of Peace will fly in ecstasy! Sweet Doves!

WHAT REALLY MATTERS TODAY, MY DEAR?

What will happen when the clock runs out of time?
It could happen at any age … yours, or mine,
And I don't mean our clock; I mean civilization's clock.
Would that be a shock?
What would it matter? No one would know.
Who would care if the birds no longer flew and the grass didn't grow?
In any era, the end for all could be hovering near.
With that in mind, I'll ask again …

WHAT REALLY MATTERS TODAY, MY DEAR?

"LIFE"

Tick, tock, tick, tock,
Day, night, day, night,
Tick, tock, tick, tock,
Seconds, minutes, seconds, minutes,
Tick, tock, tick, tock,
Minutes, hours, minutes, hours,
Tick, tock, tick, tock,
Hours, days, hours, days,
Tick, tock, tick, tock,
Days, weeks, days, weeks,
Tick, tock, tick, tock,
Weeks, months, weeks, months,
Tick, tock, tick, tock,
Months, years, months, years,
Tick, tock, tick, tock,
Day, night, day, night,
Tick, tock, tick, tock,

Tick ...